D1217626

Egyptian Mythology

A Fascinating Guide to Understanding the Gods, Goddesses, Monsters, and Mortals

© Copyright 2017

All rights reserved. No part of this book may be reproduced in any form without permission in writing from the author. Reviewers may quote brief passages in reviews.

Disclaimer: No part of this publication may be reproduced or transmitted in any form or by any means, mechanical or electronic, including photocopying or recording, or by any information storage and retrieval system, or transmitted by email without permission in writing from the publisher.

While all attempts have been made to verify the information provided in this publication, neither the author nor the publisher assumes any responsibility for errors, omissions, or contrary interpretations of the subject matter herein.

This book is for entertainment purposes only. The views expressed are those of the author alone, and should not be taken as expert instruction or commands. The reader is responsible for his or her own actions.

Adherence to all applicable laws and regulations, including international, federal, state, and local laws governing professional licensing, business practices, advertising, and all other aspects of doing business in the US, Canada, UK, or any other jurisdiction is the sole responsibility of the purchaser or reader.

Neither the author nor the publisher assumes any responsibility or liability whatsoever on the behalf of the purchaser or reader of these materials. Any perceived slight of any individual or organization is purely unintentional.

Contents

Bonus from Captivating History (limited time)

Hi History Lover!

My name is Matt Clayton, and I'm the creator of Captivating History. First off, I want to THANK YOU for reading my books in the Captivating History series. As an avid reader of History myself, I aim to produce books that will hold you captive.

Now you have a chance to join our exclusive history list so you can get at least one history ebook for free as well as discounts and a potential to get more history books for free! Simply go to

www.captivatinghistory.com/ebook

Also, make sure to follow us on:

Twitter: @Captivhistory

Facebook: Captivating History: @captivatinghistory

If you have any questions; reach out to me by sending an email to **matt@captivatinghistory.com**

Introduction

From what we know of history, Egypt, along with Sumer, were the foundations of civilization. The Fertile Crescent, which stretched from the Nile Valley to the twin rivers in Mesopotamia, gave us our earliest glimpse of organized man. But organized how? For one, both locations gave us writing—hieroglyphics in Egypt and cuneiform in Sumer. There still some debate about who was first.

In this book, we will start by looking at the gods and goddesses of Kemet—Ancient Egypt. Then, we will turn our attention to the monsters which likely gave them nightmares and humbled them in their quest to bring order to the world around them. Finally, we will look at the mortals which shaped their civilization and made Egypt the bedrock of our own history. Though Egypt today is only a third-world nation, struggling with terrorism and poverty, their heritage remains vital to the understanding of who we are as a species.

Part 1 — The Gods Come to Egypt

The Book of Knowing The Evolutions Of Ra, and of Overthrowing Apep.

[These are] the; words which the god Neb-er-tcher spake after he had, come into being:

"I am he who came into being in the form of the god Khepera, and I am the creator of that which came into being, that is to say, I am the creator of everything which came into being: now the things which I created, and which came forth out of my mouth after that I had come into being myself were exceedingly many. The sky (or heaven) had not come into being, the earth did not exist, and the children of the earth, and the creeping, things, had not been made at that time. I myself raised them up from out of Nu, from a state of helpless inertness. I found no place whereon I could stand. I worked a charm upon my own heart (or, will), I laid the foundation [of things] by Maat, and I made everything which had form. I was [then] one by myself, for I had not emitted from myself the god Shu, and I had not spit out from myself the goddess

Tefnut; and there existed no other who could work with me."

Legends of the Gods (1912)
E. A. Wallis Budge
Egyptologist and Philologist for the British Museum

Chapter 1 — Osiris, Isis, Seth, and Horus

Perhaps the most important myth of Ancient Egypt is that of Osiris. In it, his wife Isis and his son Horus battled against his brother Seth.

The spellings with which we are most familiar are modern versions of the Greek. The original Egyptian names were more like the following:

- Osiris—Auser
- Isis—Asett
- Seth—Sett
- Horus—Heru

The double "t" at the end of Asett and Sett is not traditional, but it helps to distinguish the name "Sett" from the common English word "set."

Throughout all of Egyptian myth, there is very little actually said about Osiris (Auser) himself. Most of what is said comes after his betrayal by Seth (Sett).

Imagining the Osiris Myth

As they had done for all the ages of man, the priests of the great city of Iunu had crossed over the Ne'weya during the twilight hour after dawn and before sunrise. But this morning vigil at the temple plateau was more somber than usual. All of Kemet was in mourning for their dead ruler, Auser.

The death of a god was not to be taken lightly. Such things tended to throw the entire universe out of balance. Sett had gone over to the dark side of reality. No longer did he stand on the prow of the sun barge, fighting off Apep—the great snake of chaos. Instead, Sett had become chaos. He had betrayed his brother, Auser, and had murdered him. If the priests could believe the rumors, Sett had hacked up Auser's body and flung the parts all up and down the great Ne'weya and its life-giving waters.

As the eastern horizon brightened, the priests performed their daily ritual, burning a handful of grain in sacrifice to the great god, Ra—giver of light. His return to the skies above the mortal realm would be to look upon a world greatly saddened by what had happened to the children of Geb (Earth) and Nut (Heavens). Their offspring, Auser, had been murdered by his brother, Sett. And their offspring, Asett, had been made a widow by the same action.

When the priests had returned to Iunu, they heard the news that Sett had taken control of all Kemet. Asett, Auser's lovely wife, had fled into the hills to the West. Or so people were being told.

Ahmose of Zau made his way into the temple and toward the large meeting hall. Outside the hall, he saw a familiar face. At first, he could not put a name to that visage. Something about it all didn't make sense. What was a beggar doing in the temple at this hour? And why would he recognize a beggar? Then, the truth struck him. That was no beggar, despite the shabby clothes she wore. That was Asett, herself! The goddess was in disguise.

"Your eminence!" said Ahmose, loud enough only to be heard by her. "What are you doing here? It's not safe!"

She turned and bade him to come closer.

"I need your help," she said. "Sett has robbed us all, but especially me. Auser and I wanted to have a son. If we act quickly, it is still not too late. I need for the priesthood to gather all the pieces of Auser. They are to bring them together so that I may perform sacred rites and to consummate the union which was denied us. Our son will become the rightful ruler of Kemet."

Ahmose looked confused, but nodded slowly.

"Why do you hesitate?" she asked.

"I don't doubt your powers, eminence. It's just that Sett is undoubtedly looking for you and I fear for your safety."

"What do you suggest?"

"I am from Zau, here in the Delta. I know of several places where we could bring together the pieces of your husband and find the peace and security required for your ceremony."

"Good. And thank you ..."

"Ahmose, your eminence. My name is Ahmose. I'll see to it right away." He turned to leave.

"One more thing," said Asett. "We also need to have Auser's royal accessories. Do you know of someone who can steal them away from Sett and his forces?"

Ahmose thought for a moment and nodded. "Yes, your eminence. I know of some officers who are still loyal to you and to Auser."

"Thank you, Ahmose."

"My lady." The priest hesitated. "Has Sett become corrupted by Apep?"

The goddess shook her head. "I don't know, yet. Perhaps. He had held that duty for so long, fending off the attacks of chaos. Others have taken over those duties. We can only hope they do as good a job without becoming corrupted."

Within days, all of the pieces had been returned to Lower Kemet and Ahmose had found a warehouse in Zau perfect for the sacred ceremony to be performed.

Within the week, the new god, Heru, had been born, with all the attributes needed to rule. The young god had all the skills of the father and the wisdom of the mother. In addition, Heru had the gift of sight, like his namesake—capable of seeing clearly everything from afar. And like the falcon after which he had been named, Heru also had the swiftness to strike hard at his enemies.

In the first month after his birth, Heru held many battles against his uncle. The young god was so successful in waging combat that Sett feared he might lose the war.

Ever wanting to find an advantage, Sett challenged young Heru to a battle under water.

"We should become as hippopotami and face each other beneath the waves. If either one of us surfaces before three months are up, we will forfeit. Are we agreed?"

To Heru, this seemed reasonable. Soon, they were under water battling against one another.

Asett feared for her son's life and vowed to help him win. From the sky, she hurled massive harpoons at the hippopotamus below, but she had struck the wrong beast.

Heru cried out, "Mother, you have struck me. Please be more careful with your aim."

Asett studied the scene more carefully and soon realized that her son was in pursuit of Sett. There her brother was, several dozen meters ahead.

Several times, she took careful aim, but the harpoon glanced off Sett's wet body. But finally, a harpoon stuck and Sett surfaced.

"Please, dear sister," said Sett, "take pity on your poor brother."

Asett showed her brother mercy and let him heal from his wounds.

Later, Heru confronted his mother. "How could you show him mercy after he tried so many times to kill me?" Suddenly, Heru cut off his mother's head and hid it from her in the mountains to the West.

When Ra, the sun god, heard what Heru had done to his mother, he bound the young god's hands and restored to Asett her head. Then, he gave her a crown of protection so that no one could ever do to her what Heru had done.

But while Heru was bound, Sett swooped in to take advantage of his enemy. Abruptly, he plucked out Heru's eyes and made him blind.

Asett forgave her son for what he had done and wept at what had happened to his eyes. She consulted with Tehuty, the god of wisdom and knowledge. There, she learned that new eyes could be fashioned for Heru from the old arts. Soon, Heru could see again. Once more, he went on the offensive, taking every opportunity to beat his uncle in battle.

Again, it looked as though Sett would lose everything, partly because his sister, Asett, was interfering in his war against Heru.

Sett made his way to the great council of gods—the Ennead. There, he begged the council for a meeting to discuss with Heru their differences, but without the interference of Asett.

They agreed to a meeting. So, Sett sent out word to Heru that he wanted to meet at the Island of the Middle Ground and let the Ennead judge between them. And Sett commanded the ferryman not to let anyone of the likeness of Asett to journey to that island.

The following day, the council met. There, Sett and Heru presented their cases while the council listened. In the meantime, Asett disguised herself as an old woman and bribed the ferryman with a gold ring so that she may pass to the Island of the Middle Ground.

When she arrived, she turned herself into a young maiden so that she could distract Sett and help him to fail. As she served the guests more wine, she caught Sett's eye and he called her near.

"My Lord Sett," she said. "I am so grateful for all you have done. Your bravery makes my own hardship seem more durable."

"Hardship?" replied Sett with concern. "What could make such a beautiful woman less than happy?"

"An intruder has invaded my home, killed my husband, and stolen my son's birthright."

"Damn him!" exclaimed Sett. "The man should be publicly executed for his crimes. We shall do that immediately."

"No, please!" she replied. "Do not kill him. I would never wish to have anyone's blood on my own hands. Banishing him from the land would be sufficient to set my heart at ease."

"Then," said Sett loudly, "he shall be banished."

"Thank you, my Lord Sett. For the home is Kemet, my husband was Auser, my son is Heru, and the intruder to be banished is you!"

Suddenly, Sett realized that this young wench was none other than his pesky sister. His own words had condemned himself and all in front of Heru and the gods of the Ennead. He was outraged.

Asett flew away, calling out her words to mock her brother. "You have condemned yourself, dear brother. What say you?"

"The ferryman should be punished," said Sett. So, the next day, Sett had the toes on both the ferryman's feet cut off because he had disobeyed Sett's command not to let Asett across.

Heru soon won the war and banished Sett from Kemet for all time.

Chapter 2 — The Sun and Creation

Similar to the myths of some other cultures, Egyptian creation stories talk of a time before creation which was filled with void and chaos—an expanse called "Nu."

To the Egyptians, the beginning of all things was *Zep Tepi* ("first occasion"). The void itself was described as a primordial body of water out of which rose up a mound shaped like a pyramid—a *benben*. This word is similar to the name given to the sacred bird of rebirth (compare Greek phoenix), the bennu.

From the ancient city of Khemenu (known to the late Greek rulers of Egypt as Hermopolis), their story of creation starts with the formation of eight gods of the Ogdoad.

Nu was male and his female mate was Naunet. Together, they represented the dead, primordial sea.

Huh was male and his female mate was Hauhet. Together, they represented the infinite expanse of that ancient sea.

Kuk was male and his female mate was Kauket. Together, they represented the dim murkiness which was a natural part of that primeval fluid.

Amun was male and his female mate was Amaunet. Together, they represented the opaque obscurity of that earliest of waters. This quality made it impossible to discover more about the water's nature.

With all of them filled with the theme of water, it should be no surprise that they were symbolized as frogs (male) and water snakes (female).

When the Ogdoad came together, an imbalance was created which forced the emergence of the first benben, and from it, the appearance of the sun to give its light to all of material existence.

From the ancient city of Iunu (known to the late Greek rulers of Egypt as Heliopolis), the creation story takes on a somewhat different form.

To the people of Iunu, Atum created himself out of the watery void. In some versions, Atum is seen sitting on the primordial benben; in others, he is the benben itself. Atum represented the setting sun—where the day reaches its completion.

It's interesting to note that the Hebrews also viewed sunset as the end of the day and the moment after the sun disappears as the beginning of a new day.

Because of Atum's association with the sun, he was sometimes called Ra or Atum-Ra. Like many of the myths in other cultures, the gods are frequently described as if they have human-like form. For instance, Atum either masturbates or sneezes his first two children into existence. They are the god of air, Shu, and the goddess of moisture, Tefnut.

The First Tragedy in Creation

While Atum was working on one of his many creation projects, both Shu and Tefnut took an interest in their environment.

"What is this watery substance surrounding the island of creation?" asked Shu.

"Father did not say much about it. Only that it was here before he arrived."

"Aren't you curious about it?"

"Well," replied Tefnut, "perhaps a little. What did you have in mind?"

"Father's busy. We shouldn't disturb him." Shu nodded, gaining confidence in his new decision. "Perhaps we should explore it. Maybe, if we find something of value out there, we can bring it back to Father for him to use."

Tefnut smiled and also nodded. Abruptly, she jumped into the primordial waters and swam away. Shu followed close behind.

Later, when Atum was ready for a break, he called for his children, but did not hear a reply. Soon, he became frantic. Creation was still brand new and Atum was still learning how to deal with the nature of reality and how to shape its form. Was there something he had missed? Could there be something in the tools with which he was working that created destruction? Then, he noticed a residual swirl in the primordial waters. In an instant, he knew his children had dove into those waters and had swum away.

"Oh! My dear children." He feared that they might become lost in the murky gloom of that infinite void. His light would not reach infinity. They would not be able to see it if they swam too far.

"What to do?"

All of a sudden, thought and action became one. He plucked out his right eye and cast it into the void. "Find my children!" was the commandment and divine intention.

Not long afterward, this new goddess—the Eye of Ra—returned with the children in tow.

Atum was so relieved that he wept and each teardrop became a new creation, each one an individual human being.

The Supreme Council of Gods

After Atum had worked a while at creating the world and many of the new gods he had needed to help manage all of physical reality, he established a supreme council of gods called the Ennead. Its nine members were Atum-Ra and his two children, Shu and Tefnut, and their two children, Geb and Nut, and their four children, Auser, Asett, Sett, and Nephthys.

In contrast to the Ogdoad, which dealt primarily with the void of chaos, the Ennead handled physical existence.

More Creation Stories

From the ancient city of Inbu-Hedj (known to the late Greek rulers of Egypt as Memphis), their story of creation involves the patron god of all craftsmen, Ptah. Here, the physical world was carefully crafted with intellectual precision, unlike the accident of Khemenu's creation myth, or the sneeze of Iunu's creation story.

Ptah possessed an innate ability to see a desired end result in all its details and to find all the necessary resources for its fabrication.

Egyptian myth placed the mental faculties in the heart, rather than in the brain. It was said that when Ptah spoke from the heart, the things he visualized became manifest in physical reality. As he would speak the name of something, it would suddenly appear. His spoken word was the source of all other gods, physical objects, and mortal beings.

At creation, Ptah was connected to Tatjenen, the god of the first benben.

In some respects, Ptah is similar to the Abrahamic God of Judaism and Christianity where creation was more an activity of intelligent intention. In some other respects, Ptah's method of creation—from the heart—mimics the nature of prayer. Philosopher Rod Martin, Jr. notes, "Prayer, when done right, comes from feeling or 'the heart.' It never comes from thought or the words on someone's lips. A fearful heart, asking for salvation, will receive more to fear. A confident, but humble heart, asking for anything, will receive that thing instantly. And most people are not too confident about instantly, so time (delay) becomes part of the delivery."

From the ancient city of Waset (known to the late Greek rulers of Egypt as Thebes, and in modern times, Luxor), we receive still another version of creation. To them, Amun was an invisible force behind every aspect of creation and also an element of the Ogdoad. Amun's form encompassed everything—from beyond the deepest underworld, and the highest of the heavens.

When Amun uttered his first cry, it shattered the sameness of the infinite nothingness and gave birth to both the Ogdoad, and its eight gods, but also the Ennead, and its nine gods.

To the people of Waset, Amun was a mystery shrouded in darkness for even all of the other gods. And the attributes and skills of all the other gods were merely one aspect or another of Amun. The inhabitants of Waset considered their city to be the location of the original benben.

The Sun—A Pivotal Aspect of Creation

Central to all of these stories is the appearance of the sun. All of Kemet (Egypt) worshiped at least one aspect of the sun. In fact, Heliopolis was literally "sun city."

When Atum plucked out his eye in order to find his children, Shu and Tefnut, that new goddess not only had the ability to perceive, but also the ability to cast the necessary light on her surroundings in order to see more clearly. The Eye of Ra has been represented throughout Egyptian myth by various goddesses. The list is long and includes Bastet, Hathor, Mut, Sekhmet, and Wadjet. This "eye" was sometimes symbolically represented as the solar disk. On the back of the American dollar, it may also be the eye in the benben that is glowing above a truncated pyramid.

A number of gods were more directly associated with the sun. Of course, there is Ra, who represented the sun at or near zenith, when its blazing light does most of its work in nourishing the plants of the physical world.

Naturally, the sun has different aspects to its daily cycle. Khepri took the first visible slot of the day as the sun rose. Because of this "newborn" state, he also represented rebirth.

The lesser god, Aten, represented the perceptible disk of the sun, but not any of its life-giving warmth or light.

As we've already seen, Atum represented the setting sun, which ties in thematically with his status as a source of creation. The setting sun completes each day, and Atum was able to complete each creation by giving it form, substance, and persistence.

And Ptah was long associated with the sun after it set. During each night, the sun replenished itself, preparing for the new day. Besides his skills as a craftsman, Ptah was also a god of the arts and biological creation (fertility).

Chapter 3 — Gods and Humans

As we saw earlier, humans had not remained satisfied with the status quo. To a few upstarts, harmony was boring. Those few wanted something more. They were not content to follow Maat, the goddess of order.

Ra was no fool. He realized that humans would one day get restless and attempt something similarly stupid. Up until that time, life had existed in a state of perpetual sameness called *djet*. By creating a dichotomous existence called *neheh,* his mortal children would have some variety to their existence. They would have day and night, the monthly cycles, and the seasons of the year.

Ra also reasoned that having his rule on Earth made him and his court a tempting target. Because of this, Ra made another drastic change.

"Shu?"

"Yes, my Lord Father."

"As god of the air, I want you ..."—Ra turned to the others of court waiting in attendance—"... and you, you, all eight of you. I want you all to lift up Nut, goddess of the sky. Hold her aloft so that we can reside far above the humans."

"Because of their selfishness?" asked Tefnut.

"Yes, my darling child. The human selfishness will now have no way to reach us."

"But can we rule the world effectively from such a distance?" asked Sett, one of the sons of Nut.

"I'm glad you brought that up," replied Ra. "Because you've been busy helping me ferry the sun across the sky, I will give the job of local rule to your brother, Auser. He and his wife, Asett, will take charge of Kemet and manage affairs there. We'll never be far away and we can all move in to intervene, if needed."

Auser stepped forward and asked, "Lord Ra, do you have any advice for me before I begin my task?"

"Keep the order of things. The society of Kemet shall remain rigid. Every individual is to do that to which they were assigned and into that which they were born. To vary from this is to invite chaos. Without this control, all manner of surprising things could happen. We cannot allow great change. I have given them enough variety with the days, the months, and the yearly cycles."

And so, Nut was lifted into the sky and the gods ruled from on high. Auser descended to Kemet and took charge of the land as Ra had commanded. But humans were not the only ones who felt the lure of temptation.

As Auser and Asett left the presence of the other gods, Sett looked on and wished he had that job, instead of standing on the prow of the sun barge every day, hacking at each threat from Apep.

Part 2 — Monsters of Egypt

"Apep, the serpent-devil of mist, darkness, storm, and night, of whom more will be said later on, and his fiends, the 'children of rebellion,' were not the result of the imagination of the Egyptians in historic times, but their existence dates from the period when Egypt was overrun by mighty beasts, huge serpents, and noxious reptiles of all kinds. The great serpent of Egyptian mythology, which was indeed a formidable opponent of the Sun-god, had its prototype in some monster serpent on earth, of which tradition had preserved a record; and that this is no mere theory is proved by the fact that the remains of a serpent, which must have been of enormous size, have recently been found in the Fayyum."

E. A. Wallis Budge
Keeper of the Egyptian and Assyrian
Antiquities in the British Museum
The Gods of the Egyptians, vol.I, 1904

Chapter 4 — Apep: Great Snake of Chaos

There weren't too many true monsters in Egyptian mythology, unlike the myths of many other cultures. The Norse had their Kraken and great wolf, Fenrir. The Greeks had their Scylla, Charybdis, Echidna, and Typhon. In Egypt's lore, the only true monster was chaos which took the form of a giant snake. Its name was Apep (Apophis in Ancient Greek). We will look more closely at this creature in a moment.

Fearsome Gods of Egypt

Many of the gods of Egyptian mythology could, at times, be fearsome, but quite often it was to the enemies of Egypt (Kemet) or to those who had done great evil.

For instance, Am-heh, with a name that meant either "eater of eternity" or "devourer of millions," had the head of a dog and body of a human, and lived on a lake of flame in the underworld. If you got on his bad side, no one but the god Atum-Ra could calm him down. But this was only another reason to live a good and righteous life.

Early in the history of the universe, Ra discovered that his mortal children—humans—had grown dissatisfied with peace and order. They wanted to overthrow Ra, the ruler of the universe, and were plotting to take his place. This deeply troubled Ra that his creation would be working with chaos to upend the order of things.

"What shall I do?" Ra asked of his fellow gods. "It's all I and Sett can do to hold off Apep when I bring light to the world each day."

"What should we do with anyone who threatens creation?" asked Hathor. "A criminal must be punished."

"Or eliminated," said Shu.

Ra brooded for a moment and finally nodded, turning to Hathor. "Do you have a suggestion?"

Hathor started to reply, but Tefnut spoke instead. "Hathor's daughter, Sekhmet, could slaughter them. She seems well suited for that kind of task. As a lioness, she can hunt them down and devour them."

Ra took a deep breath and said, "Sekhmet, come forth. I have need of your talents."

The lion goddess moved forward to stand before Ra. "Yes, your eminence. How may I serve you?"

"The humans have become egocentric. Their selfishness threatens the very fabric of all creation. I want you to devour them all. Remove their kind from the world."

"I understand, Lord Ra. But do you realize that once I start, the bloodlust will blind me to any other needs and plug my ears to any other requests?"

"I understand," replied Ra. "Let it be done. Begin now."

So, Sekhmet turned from the Ennead and all those gathered in attendance. She went out to the world at large and began slaughtering every human that she could find—man, woman, and child. With her claws, she slashed at their bodies, spilling their blood over everything. She would wallow in that blood and then drink it up. The carnage had begun.

The following day, as Ra moved the sun across the sky, with Sett at the prow of his barge to fend off Apep, he looked down at the world. From even there, he could hear the wailing. He could smell the fear and death.

"Tehuty?" said Ra, turning to the god of wisdom and knowledge. "What do you think of this thing that Sekhmet does below us?"

"While it is true that many of the humans were plotting to overthrow the gods, including you, my Lord, there were some who possessed righteous hearts. Certainly, those who held chaos in their hearts should be punished, but—"

"But you think it was wrong to kill them all."

Tehuty nodded.

"And Maat? What do you say about all this?"

The goddess of order took several moments to gather her thoughts before speaking. She knew that quick words could create their own chaos. "My Lord, what you have started has its own wisdom. Certainly, the humans have now grown fearful of the gods and many have become repentant for their conspiracies. And I agree that a few were never so treasonous as to deserve such a painful death. If only there were some way to keep a few of the humans to see if the threat of extinction has made them sufficiently humble."

"But how?" asked Ra. "Sekhmet said herself that she is unstoppable now that she has started drinking up the blood. Would it be valuable to save a few? They had such potential."

Tehuty nodded. "Saving a few, my Lord, would be a good thing. How? Perhaps we could make Sekhmet drunk so that she would forget her bloodlust."

Ra laughed and shook his head. "Brilliant suggestion, but how would you carry it out? I don't see her slowing down to indulge in such things."

"She seeks only blood," said Sett. "Give her more blood."

"Yes," said Ra. "Make seven thousand jugs of beer. Thicken them and add a color to make them look much as blood. Then pour the beer onto the land before her so that she drinks it up instead of the blood."

By the next day, the jugs of beer had been brewed, thickened, and colored. All of the gods helped to pour the red liquid before the rampaging Sekhmet. Sure enough, she stopped to drink it all and when she was done, she walked a few more paces and sleepily lay down to rest. When she awoke, Ra was there to give her a new command.

"My dearest Sekhmet," said Ra.

"My Lord," she replied, looking away as if burdened by a considerable guilt. "I feel my task is not yet complete."

"But it is," said Ra. "You have done well and I now need a few of the humans to remain alive so that they may learn humility from what you have accomplished."

"I understand."

And so, Sekhmet had become a scourge to humanity, but only for a brief while. Mankind had called her wrath upon itself.

The Meaning of Apep

Before creation, all was chaos—without form or purpose. This was known as Apep, and it took the form of a giant snake.

It was the job of the gods to dispel the darkness of chaos and to replace it with order and light.

Occasionally, Sett would become overwhelmed while attending to the prow on Ra's barge. Apep would attempt to swallow the sun, blotting out its light, but always Sett would regain control of the situation, repel Apep and restore the light of the sun.

In the world of reason and science, we know that the "swallowing" of the sun was merely an occurrence of a solar eclipse by the Moon. The order of our physical universe is merely the result of physical law's constancy and continuity.

Throughout Egyptian history, the pharaohs were agents of the sun in dispelling the chaos of the uncivilized folk who were always attempting to invade their lands. In many ways, those uncivilized people were agents of Apep, destroying the order of things. Thus, all of the Egyptian gods were monsters to the enemies of Kemet and to the instruments of Apep.

Chapter 5 — Sett: God of Desert, Storms, War, Evil, and Chaos

Sett was not always a bad guy. Originally, he was a member of the Ennead—the council of gods.

After Sekhmet had destroyed most of humanity, Ra had the gods lift Nut (sky) far from the Earth. There, the gods would rule over the world from afar. In order to maintain order locally, however, Ra set Auser (Osiris) as ruler over Kemet and Asett, as his wife, to rule with him.

Sett grew jealous, for even the gods were not above becoming self-centered and selfish. One might wonder if Sett had had too many close calls with Apep. Had he become tainted with Apep's intent—to subvert order with chaos?

So, throughout all of Egyptian myth, only Apep and Sett may be considered true monsters, for their intent was against that of peace and order, and toward self-concern and selfish need.

Seduced by Power and the Dark Side

A new day had begun. Ra was once again commanding his barge across the sky, towing the image and likeness of the sun to shine its light upon the world below. With him were Maat, the goddess of order, and Tehuty, the god of wisdom and knowledge. At the prow stood Sett, sword at the ready to strike against Apep should the great serpent attempt to interfere.

The sameness of this event made Sett a little crazy. Here he was, perched on the divine barge, doing the same thing over and over again, every day of the year, and every year, one after the other.

Below, he could see the humans and their varied activities. Some were coming together to build their separate civilizations. Sett admired the activity and the consequences of such building. He liked the sense of change and progress.

Then, Sett caught a glimpse of Asett and Auser, ruling over the greatest nation of the world—Kemet. The ribbon of water, which snaked through the desert, glistened as it reflected the sun's light back up at him and at the other members of the divine barge.

"What is it like to rule?" he wondered. "What is it like to command others and to have them do your bidding?"

And as he wondered, he didn't see that Apep was circling the barge, looking for an opportunity to strike.

"Sett!" yelled Ra. "What are you doing? Apep has taken a bite out of the sun."

The younger god blinked several times and looked back toward the sun. Indeed, part of it had already become darkened and in the glare of the light that remained, he could see the shadowy form of Chaos writhing through the sky. Immediately, he struck at the beast, but it would not let go.

The sky became increasingly dark until all of the sun's light had been snuffed out. Repeatedly, Sett struck at the beast and finally drove his blade into its heart. Slowly, Apep gave up its prize and light returned to the world.

Minutes later, he could see the eternal snake slithering away across the universe.

"Well done, my son," said Ra. "Again, you have prevailed against Chaos."

Sett nodded at the praise, but felt empty. Moments before, he had felt his own heart pounding with the excitement of conflict in action. Now, all returned to the sameness of boring order and tranquility.

Why couldn't I have more conflict in my life? Sett asked of himself. To feel the excitement of a life-threatening challenge.

As Sett mulled over these dark thoughts, his eyes drifted once again down to the Great Hall from where Auser ruled over all of Kemet. "If I had his power, I'd use it to conquer other lands. That would be enough excitement to last several millennia."

Later, as the day came to its completion, and the divine barge was taken over by the maintenance crews of the night, Sett wandered toward Kemet to pay his brother and sister a visit. The closer he got, the darker his heart became, and the more he resented that they had what he now desperately wanted.

The god of defense had now been seduced by the desire to attack. Halfway to Kemet, he stopped. There, in the bright, starlit desert, he pondered how he might achieve his deepest desires. But betrayal would not be easy. The remainder of the night he spent plotting against his brother and sister.

As the clarion call came for him to return to the divine barge, he looked down at his right arm and felt the blood coursing through his own veins. In his mind's eye, he could see Apep swimming through his veins, giving his life new meaning.

Over the next several weeks, Sett talked in veiled language to many of the lesser gods and to some of the more powerful humans of Kemet. From his many conversations, he was able to discern the hearts of those who would be willing to help him in his quest for power. Over those many days, he built an army of like-minded who desired change—the same magnitude of change which had turned the universe from a realm of chaos into one of order.

Then, one day, Sett did not show up when the call came to board the barge of the sun.

"Where is Sett?" asked Ra.

"I do not know, my Lord," replied Tehuty.

"Neither do I," said Maat. "What will we do?"

"We will take turns warding off Apep," said Ra with growing certainty. "We must maintain the order of time. The day must have its period of sunlight. We will find Sett later, when our work in the sky is done."

About mid-morning, Tehuty was standing guard at the prow of the barge when he was distracted by a flurry of motion below.

"Ra!" he shouted. "Look! It's Sett. He's attacking Kemet."

Ra looked down in horror as Sett and his mighty forces swept across Kemet, destroying the armies of Auser.

And as Sett approached the capital city, Auser came out to meet with his brother.

"Why do you do this, brother?" asked Auser. "Why aren't you on the divine barge guarding the sun?"

A dark smirk crossed Sett's face as he replied, "Just as Ra saw the changes that brought order to the universe, I am overseeing the changes that will demonstrate power and control in the universe."

"At what cost?" asked Auser. "You are destroying order. Apep will surely have an advantage if you continue."

"I know how to handle Apep," said Sett. "After all, I've been fighting back chaos for thousands of years. No one is more qualified than I."

"But—"

"Take him!" commanded Sett.

And the minions of Sett took Auser and bound him.

"Brother, I do this for the good of the universe." Abruptly, Sett began hacking at his brother's body, cutting it into more than a dozen pieces. Then, he turned to his chiefs and commanded them, "Each of you take a piece of my brother and take it to a major city of Kemet. This way, Auser will no longer have power over Kemet."

The rest of the gods were shocked by what Sett had done, but his bold actions also engendered for him a measure of respect from nearly all of the divine beings. The only one not so touched by admiration was, of course, Auser's sister and wife, Asett.

Part 3 — Egyptian Mortals Who Shaped History

Ozymandias

I met a traveller from an antique land,
Who said—"Two vast and trunkless legs of stone
Stand in the desert. . . . Near them, on the sand,
Half sunk a shattered visage lies, whose frown,
And wrinkled lip, and sneer of cold command,
Tell that its sculptor well those passions read
Which yet survive, stamped on these lifeless things,
The hand that mocked them, and the heart that fed;
And on the pedestal, these words appear:
My name is Ozymandias, King of Kings;
Look on my Works, ye Mighty, and despair!
Nothing beside remains. Round the decay
Of that colossal Wreck, boundless and bare
The lone and level sands stretch far away."

—Percy Bysshe Shelley, 1818, *The Examiner* of London

Chapter 6 — Imhotep, the 27th Century BC Polymath

Five hundred years after what modern historians call the "First Dynasty"—after the first Scorpion King—and nearly four hundred years after Narmer the Great had unified all of Kemet, Djoser ruled the land of the sacred river. He ruled from Inbu-Hedj ("the white walls"), a city that would be known to the Greeks as Memphis.

A man named Imhotep assisted the pharaoh and proved to be so indispensable that he had earned the right to be called "first in line after the king."

Kenneth Feder, anthropologist and professor of archaeology, lists the official titles of Imhotep in one of his books: "Chancellor of the King of Egypt, Doctor, First in line after the King of Upper Egypt, Administrator of the Great Palace, Hereditary nobleman, High Priest of Heliopolis, Builder, Chief Carpenter, Chief Sculptor, and Maker of Vases in Chief."

Imhotep was also a poet and philosopher who was frequently quoted throughout most of Egyptian history.

So, it seems, Imhotep was what we would call a polymath, or "Renaissance man." His knowledge was broad, stretching across many fields. His skills were varied and of great depth, so that he may be compared favorably with the likes of Leonardo da Vinci, Galileo Galilei, and Johann Wolfgang von Goethe.

This right-hand man to the king was also a mathematician, astronomer, and architect. It is said that he designed the first pyramid—the Step Pyramid at Saqqara.

By the time of the Roman Republic, Imhotep had been elevated to the status of a god. His medical works were used during the Roman Empire and were so highly thought of that two Roman emperors (Tiberius and Claudius) had temple inscriptions include praise for Imhotep.

Imhotep the Master Planner

The king's chancellor went to bed tired, but happy. He had accomplished a great many things with his time in service to all of Kemet and to the resident god, Djoser, emissary of Heru, and representative of the Ennead on Earth.

Outside his darkened bedroom, the stars filled the sky with a warm glow. Unlike most men, Imhotep looked at every part of existence as a resource and as a source of solutions. While the field of stars held the world, he held his wife and drifted off into a deep sleep.

During his dreams, he remembered the concern discussed by his king earlier in the day—that the grain harvest this year was noticeably less than that of the previous year. Then, as dreams so easily do, he turned once and found himself seven years into the future, after as many years of plenty. The people were becoming fat with prosperity. He turned once more and found himself another seven years into the future, but this time many of his people were dead or dying. Those who remained were thin from starvation.

The next moment, he found himself sitting upright in bed. The bedding was cold and clinging. Sweat dripped down his face from the anguish he had felt moments before.

"What is it, my love?" asked his wife. "Is something wrong?"

"No, my beloved. Go back to sleep. Everything is as it should be."

The chancellor got up and crossed the room to the outer hall. So as not to awaken his wife, he called quietly to his slave, "Fetch a flame for my lantern. I need to write some notes for the coming daylight."

In moments, the slave had returned and lit Imhotep's lantern and the chancellor then went to his study to write down the thoughts that were coming to him.

For a moment, he sat there merely looking at the papyrus and the reed pen he held, ready for ink.

"Look at the problem," he whispered to himself. "What exactly is its nature? What is there behind the feeling I have?"

He nodded. "Famine. Prevention."

Quickly, he opened the small clay jar and dipped his reed pen into it, drawing into it some of the ink. Deftly, he stroked the papyrus surface, combining the symbols which grew in meaning to match the thoughts in his mind. In moments, he had captured the gist of his concerns and had made a list of possible solutions. The most promising such solution seemed to be that of storing surplus in years of plenty and rationing that storage when needed.

When done, he held the papyrus sheet up and admired its contents. Such a simple idea, it's a wonder no one had considered it ever before. He half laughed at the ironic thought that this brilliant idea may have come too late. What if next year's harvest begins years of famine?

He shrugged and smiled. No sense worrying. "Worry," he whispered to himself, "is a wasted effort about something that might not happen. Better to enjoy the moments we have and to make the best of them."

With that, he took the papyrus and the lamp, and returned to his bedroom. After placing the valuable writing in a safe place on a side table, he blew out the lantern and returned to bed and to his wife.

This time, as he drifted off to sleep, he felt the happiness of that rare kind of person who always finds solutions to the problems of this mortal world. He knew his own intelligence was substantial, but that alone had not made him chancellor to King Djoser. There were others more intelligent than he, but they lacked his humble attitude and his child-like imagination.

When the sun returned the following morning, Imhotep broke his fast, then kissed his wife before leaving for the palace main.

When he arrived at the king's side, he waited until the pharaoh had finished his daily routine.

"Any new business?" Djoser asked his counselor.

"Yes, my Lord," said Imhotep. "I have a suggestion on the topic we discussed yesterday—concerning the shortage of grain harvest."

King Djoser tilted his head to the side and squinted his eyes. An expression of growing interest covered his face.

"There is a certain minimum amount we need to keep our nation healthy. I propose that we store all grain beyond that minimum until we have seven years of surplus. This way, the unpredictable nature of Nile flooding will never threaten our survival. We will always have enough to keep us alive and thriving until the years of abundance return to us."

Sudden laughter startled Imhotep. He shook his head and moved backward one step. Then, he looked upon his king's smiling face and returned his own smile.

"Very good, my friend," said Djoser. "Very, very good. My faith in you was well placed. You continue to contribute far more to Kemet than any counselor who has come before. For that reason, I hereby proclaim you to be my second-in-command. Whenever I am away, your words will be as my own. So it shall be done."

Imhotep bowed to his king and felt greatly humbled by the honor bestowed on him. He accepted the honor graciously, but inwardly prayed that he would always live up to that honor—that he would continue to have the creativity and wisdom to do for Kemet, and for his king, what needed to be done.

Chapter 7 — Akhenaten, the King Who Upended Tradition

Amenhotep IV was the second son of Amenhotep III. The father had been a highly successful pharaoh—the ninth of the Eighteenth Dynasty, reigning from 1388–1351 BC. More statues were found of the father than any other Egyptian king.

Amenhotep IV's older brother, Thutmose, was destined to be king after his father, but in the 30th year of the elder's reign, Thutmose died. Suddenly, Amenhotep IV was to become the father's successor (1351–1334). And in the 37th year of the father's rule over Egypt, the father died. All that power and prosperity went to the second son. Was there foul play? We have no way of knowing. The records about the successor are scarce.

We do know that in the fifth year of his reign, Amenhotep IV changed his name to Akhenaten. The name he had shared with his father—Amenhotep—meant "Amun is satisfied," in honor of the god whose name meant "invisible" or "the hidden one." The new name meant "effective for Aten." And Aten was a sun god, referring to the solar disk, rather than the other aspects of the sun—its light, heat, giving of life, and dividing the day from the night.

For 200 years, Amun had retained national popularity as one of Egypt's most important deities. Before that, Amun had been only a local deity. But when the city of Waset (later named Thebes by the Greeks) was made the capital of unified Egypt, what was local had become national. In those ten generations, the high priests of Amun had gained great power and influence.

Now, this one king who was not even supposed to have been king, was turning his back on this supreme god, in favor of some minor angel barely mentioned in the ancient texts.

At first, Akhenaten was tolerant of the religious beliefs of others. But gradually, he began to put more and more pressure on departing from the old ways. He used the wealth of Egypt to build a new capital which he called Akhetaten (modern Amarna) at a place where nothing had ever been built before—an entire city constructed in the wilderness from zero.

During his reign, Egypt lost a considerable area from its northern holdings to the Hittites. Some felt that this king was dabbling in chaos and that the losses were from the sins of chaos. Certainly, the Amun priests of Waset would have found this idea popular.

Akhenaten had several wives, as was the tradition of pharaohs. His Great Royal Wife, or chief consort, was Nefertiti. Other wives included Kiya, Meritaten, Ankhesenamun, and a sister whose name is unknown, but who is called "The Younger Lady" by historians.

Nefertiti gave her husband only daughters—six of them.

Imagining Akhenaten

The grand vizier moved slowly toward the throne and bowed. As he did so, he lifted up several clay tablets.

"Approach," said Akhenaten. "What do we have here?"

"Reports, my Lord," said the grand vizier. "From your vassal states in Canaan."

The king lifted his right hand and curled his fingers as if to summon the vizier to come closer. But the man knew better that the meaning was to elicit more facts.

"Yes, your eminence," said the vizier. "These are pleas from Rib-Hadda for military assistance and—"

"Again?" Akhenaten shook his head in disbelief. "That one administrator sends more messages to me than all the others combined. If he loses his position in Byblos from a coup, I will welcome it, just so long as his successor continues to pay tribute to the Empire. Right now, I'm more concerned with our campaign in Nubia. Any word from there?"

"Not yet, your eminence."

Akhenaten took a deep breath and waited a moment more. "Any other affairs of state to discuss?"

"Thankfully no, my Lord. But the Great Royal Wife and your six daughters wish to see you."

"Nefertiti," replied the king. "Yes, please. Send them in."

After Akhenaten

All in all, Akhenaten ruled Egypt for 17 years. After Akhenaten died, Smenkhkare became the new king and he ruled for something like one year. Very little is know about him, because later kings tried to erase from history every record of Akhenaten and everyone associated with him. Smenkhkare may have been a son of Akhenaten or a brother; we simply do not know.

After Smenkhkare, a woman sat on the throne. She was named Neferneferuaten. She ruled for about two years. Was she Nefertiti, or one of Akhenaten's daughters by Nefertiti (Meriaten or Neferneferuaten Tasherit)? We do not know this, either.

Imagining King Tut

All of Akhetaten was in mourning, officially, but secretly many rejoiced that another member of the sacrilegious family had died. Neferneferuaten had ruled for one year and nine months, but the priest of Amun made certain that every one of her orders had been thwarted in one fashion or another.

Some say that the stress of her inability to command finally got to her. Others say that the vizier who died at the same time had sacrificed himself in order to poison her last meal. He had tasted it, showing that it was safe, but according to some, it was a slow-acting poison that the vizier himself had used.

Today, the funeral had ended. Neferneferuaten had now been buried in her makeshift tomb. Before the crowds stood a young boy of nine. Behind him stood the new grand vizier, his assistants, plus several cousins and the boy's mother, known to historians only as The Younger

Lady. Today, Tutankhaten the boy would become King Tut, ruler over all of Kemet—from Nubia to Canaan, and from Libya to the Red Sea.

After the crowning ceremony, the vizier whisked the young boy into council chambers. Surrounding the boy were a host of counselors, scribes, and junior viziers. All of them were adherents of Amun, the one true god of Egypt—the most supreme god which had no form. Compared to him, all others were mere angels or divine servants. Even Aten was merely a part of the immortal hosts, but he was nothing compared to the father of all creation.

"Lord," said the grand vizier, "as you know, a pharaoh is divinity on Earth. You are the current divinity. Praise be to King Tutankhaten whose name means 'living image of Aten.' Three short years ago, your father ruled this land. As divinity on Earth, he failed his primary charge to support Maat on Earth to maintain order in the face of chaos. As we know, chaos is death—death for Kemet, death for all life, and death for all creation. Even Lord Aten—your namesake—would appreciate these facts."

"So, what are you saying?" asked the young king. "That my name is an abomination? That I am not worthy because I have been named after Aten rather than Amun?"

"No, my Lord," replied the grand vizier, hastily. "We will all follow you wherever you lead. Our fate is tied to your guidance. If you tell us to go to war, we will go. If you tell us to die, we will die. For the good of all Kemet is more important than the life of one individual."

"Even the life of this one, nine-year-old boy?"

"No, your eminence." The grand vizier took a deep breath. This was going to be more difficult than he had imagined. "You are no longer merely a boy. You are Kemet. Your life and well-being must be protected at all cost. Without you, there is no Kemet."

"If that is the case," said the young king, slowly, "then why was my stepmother poisoned?"

The grand vizier's face grew red. A volley of shocked expressions ran through the crowd of administrators surrounding the king. Suddenly, the naked reality confronted all of them that this young king could have all of them put to death. He could wipe the slate clean and establish a new set of advisors.

The grand vizier was wise in his years and knew that this young king had seen great turmoil in the land because of the disagreements with the policies of Akhenaten, the boy's father. He knew that he needed to take the darkness on directly.

"My Lord," he said quietly, "you have the power and authority to put all of us to death."

Those words shocked many of the advisors present. Some merely held their collective breaths and waited for the boy king's response.

"If we offend you," continued the grand vizier, "in any way, you need to take decisive action against that which damages the order of things. The old vizier was crazy, driven mad by chaos. But that's what happens when a king or queen leads Kemet toward chaos. It is your right to do that. You can utterly destroy Kemet, for Kemet is yours and yours alone. As long as we remain sane and free of chaos, we will follow your commands to the letter, even if they lead us all to chaos."

The young king took a deep breath and turned away from the grand vizier. He scanned the faces of the others, gauging their expressions. On some, he saw suppressed terror, but a resolve to obey. On others, he saw merely the quiet attitude of a courtly toady—a pasted-on smile and shrewd, penetrating eyes.

The new pharaoh turned again and faced the grand vizier. "What do you recommend?"

"Over the first few years of your long reign," replied the grand vizier, taking an even deeper breath before continuing, "I recommend that you return Kemet to the rule of Maat, goddess of order. Our land has been torn by this diversion to Aten. First, you could change your name, for that is your right as Lord of all Kemet. Something to honor Amun—the one true god."

"So," said the king, "change my name to Tutankhamun—'living image of Amun'—a god which has no image?"

"If you wish, my Lord."

"What else?"

"I recommend that we move the capital back to Waset so that our people can feel that order has been restored to the land."

"Very well," said the young king. "I will think about what you have suggested. I appreciate your candor and your wisdom. All of Kemet is blessed that it has such a strong and wise counselor. Now, leave me, so that I may think on these things."

A Return to Order

Soon, the entire city of Akhetaten was abandoned and everything there fell into ruin.

When nine years later the teenage pharaoh died, his grand uncle, Ay, took the throne. That man ruled for four brief years.

When Ay died, the chief commander of the army took over. His name was Horemheb, an appellation which meant "Horus is in jubilation." This new king ruled for fourteen years and spent a good portion of it destroying every monument left by Akhenaten. The building materials were used instead for more traditional monuments. Because of this, modern historians almost never found out about Akhenaten and his family. In fact, the king lists handed down from one pharaoh to the next showed Amenhotep III followed directly by Horemheb.

When Horemheb died, he made sure to hand the rule of the empire over to his vizier—a man named Paramesse. The vizier took the throne with the name Ramesses I—grandfather of Ramesses the Great.

Chapter 8 — Ramesses the Great

All of Egyptian history seemed to lead up to the great Ozymandias—Ramesses II (c1303–1213 BC). Everything which came after him did not measure up to his stature. He was the King of Kings—the one about whom the poet would write, some 3,000 years later: "Look on my Works, ye Mighty, and despair!" Yet, his power eventually crumbled to dust.

Ramesses II's father, Seti I, reclaimed much of the territory lost under Akhenaten. He had even taken back Kadesh (a town in Syria) and the region of Amurru, both conquered decades before by the Hittites. But the Egyptians under Seti once again lost Kadesh, because it was so close to the Hittite homelands and not easily controlled from the Egyptian capital.

In his second year on the throne, Ramesses II (reign 1279–1213 BC) was faced with a threat to commerce from the Sherden sea pirates. Other nations had been sending ships rich with cargo to Egypt for trade, but the pirates saw this as an opportunity for easy prosperity. The king placed ships and troops all along the Egyptian coast at strategic locations. He used merchant ships as bait, but each was filled with soldiers. The pirates took the bait and suffered their own enslavement.

Ramesses retook Amurru from the Hittites during his fourth year.

The king built a new capital city of Pi-Ramesses and included factories which would manufacture the tools of war—chariots, swords, shields, and more.

During his seventh year, Ramesses returned to the North to battle the Hittites once again. Though his campaign proved successful, Kadesh and Amurru were soon returned to Hittite control. In the tenth year, Ramesses attempted once again to reclaim that northern territory, but failed.

Relations between the two countries remained uneasy for several years thereafter.

Mursili III ruled the Hittite Empire from 1272–1265 BC, but was deposed by his uncle, Hattusili III, because of the younger man's lack of skill and the fact that he let the Assyrians capture their huge territory of Hanigalbat (Mittani). At first Mursili III attempted to regain the throne, but failed. When all hope for him looked lost, he fled

to the one place no Hittite would ever go—
Egypt.

Hattusili III discovered that Mursili III had
gone to Egypt and sent word to the court
of Ramesses demanding that his nephew
be returned to Hatti. The Egyptian
pharaoh denied any knowledge of Mursili
III's presence in the lands of the Nile. The
Hittite king did not believe Ramesses and
threatened war.

In the year 1258 BC—Ramesses' 21st
year—both kings agreed to draw up a
peace treaty. Neither side seemed well
equipped to pursue a perpetual war over
Kadesh, and neither side was willing
merely to walk away from the city or its
surrounding territory.

The World's First Known Peace Treaty

A tall, middle-aged man crossed the room and looked down at the table where the grand vizier stood. The vizier indicated the scroll on the table and bowed his head to the one who had approached. This was no ordinary man of 45 years. He was trim, with a bearing of confidence and power. When he moved, everyone in the room noticed. This was the King of Kings and he was being humbled by today's event.

After a few moments, Ramesses II looked up from the table. His eyes drilled into those of the vizier. "You've got to be kidding. I'm not signing this." He glanced at the Hittite representative who stood a few paces behind his vizier. "Really? Egypt sued Hatti for peace? Do you really want to start a war on the eve of peace?" He shook his head. "No! This won't do. It's all wrong. The Hittites sued for peace, not the other way around."

"Your eminence," said the Hittite. "If I may."

"Speak. It may be the last time you do, but if it can prevent war, then you must."

He shook his head again and turned away from them.

"What if we have two versions of the treaty?" The Hittite hesitated, and waited a moment to see if his first words invited more.

Ramesses turned, eyes narrowing as if to focus more sharply on the man himself.

The Hittite continued. "We both need to appease our courts and noblemen. We cannot take back a treaty which says that Hatti sued for peace. And I easily understand why you cannot take back one which says that Egypt sued for peace. Both are positions of weakness, and I know that both parties are not weak. But we must keep appearances. If we can both agree to sign a treaty with two versions of wording—everything the same except that which is needed to keep our people happy—then we will have accomplished something truly remarkable."

Ramesses nodded. "I'm beginning to appreciate the notion that diplomats are very much like salesmen in the bazaars. We need to check our valuables when we leave—to make certain we possess all our fingers. I have no doubt your skills at tricking us are mighty." He paused for a moment, then winked at his vizier. Abruptly, he turned and left.

The vizier turned to the startled Hittite and said, "Then it is agreed. Two wordings. All clauses of substance shall be exactly the same, but those which are for show only will have two versions—the Hittite version to show a favorable image of Hatti, and the Egyptian version to show a favorable image of Kemet."

The Hittite took a deep breath, nodded, and offered a guarded smile at what had been accomplished here. These men had created something the world had never before seen. He hoped that this treaty of peace would last.

Chapter 9 — Cleopatra, End of an Epoch

Alexander the Great conquered Egypt in 332 BC. This is why so many of the Egyptian cities of the Classical period had Greek names—Thebes, Memphis, Heliopolis, etc. In addition, the city of Alexandria, Egypt was founded by him. For the last 300 years of Ancient Egypt's existence, the land of the Nile was ruled by those of Greek heritage.

Cleopatra VII was the last of her dynasty—the last ruler of a sovereign, Ancient Egypt. After her, Egypt was merely a province of one empire after another—the Roman Empire(30 BC–AD 400), the Byzantine Empire (400–628), the Sasanian Empire of Persia (628–639), the Fatimid Caliphate (c650–c1250), the Mamluks (c1250–1517), the Ottoman Empire (1517–1867), and finally as a British protectorate (1882–1952).

With Cleopatra, more than three thousand years of history were coming to an end. Egypt would no longer have a pharaoh after her.

As a young girl of fourteen, Cleopatra (69–30 BC) came to power for the first time, but one of her decisions turned out to be very unpopular. By the time she had turned 21, her younger brother, Ptolemy XIII, had taken her place as sole ruler of Egypt. After a failed rebellion, Cleopatra fled the country.

About the same time, Rome was entangled in a brutal civil war between Julius Caesar and the great Pompey. When Pompey fled to Egypt and asked for assistance, Ptolemy XIII feared the consequences of any action he might take—either helping or shunning the Roman general. One of his advisors, however, suggested a third option which would help Caesar and gain his favor. So, Ptolemy ordered Pompey to be assassinated. When the pharaoh's representative presented Pompey's severed head to Caesar, the Roman was outraged that this Roman consul had been betrayed so brutally.

Caesar took over the Egyptian capital and decided to end the feud between Ptolemy and his sister, Cleopatra.

When Cleopatra heard of this, she returned to Egypt and had her agents roll her up in a carpet so that she could be taken past Ptolemy's guards into the midst of Julius Caesar. Once there, she used her charms to win Caesar's affections. Nine months later, their son, Ptolemy Caesar (47–30 BC), was born.

Both mother and son were taken to Rome as guests of Caesar. They lived there for two years, until Julius Caesar was assassinated (March 15, 44 BC). They both returned to Egypt and later that year, Cleopatra declared that her son, though only three years of age, would be co-ruler with her.

After Caesar's death, Rome was ruled by a triumvirate which included Gaius Octavius (Octavian, adopted son of Julius Caesar), Marcus Antonius (Mark Antony), and Lepidus. When Lepidus was forced into retirement in 36 BC, Octavian controlled the Western provinces, while Antony controlled those in the East. During that period, Mark Antony had three children with Cleopatra.

Imagining the Final Days of Kemet

Nearly three years had passed since the triumvirate had been broken. Octavian grew suspicious of Mark Antony, the leader of the East. When he heard that Mark Antony had declared young Caesarion (Ptolemy Caesar) to be the true heir of Julius Caesar, Octavian naturally felt threatened. He was only an adopted son; Caesarion had the great general's blood running through his veins.

"Your eminence," said the old man, "what you said in the Senate was masterful. Condemning Antony for all of the titles and grants of territory he had given to his relatives—the Senate understands these things. They fear and loathe such selfishness and arrogant nepotism. But remember, everything you do must be with humility and reverence to the traditions of Rome. You cannot be seen to seek power for yourself. You must refuse power. When it is forced upon you, you must accept it reluctantly."

Octavian had been looking out the window onto the moonlit Tyrrhenian Sea. He half heard the wisdom of his old counselor. The other half of his thoughts were on the far end of the Mediterranean, wondering how he could destroy Marcus Antonius and his evil bitch queen, Cleopatra.

"How do I kill them, Claudius?" He turned from the window and looked into the eyes of his advisor. Octavian was 29; his advisor was 69.

"You don't," said old man. "You can never be seen to have killed them. You must always be seen as magnanimous, strong, but forgiving. A few will hate you for showing leniency. You cannot please everyone. But the majority of Rome—especially the patricians and senators—will appreciate the strength it takes to show mercy."

"If I cannot kill them, then how will I ever be rid of them? This claim by Marcus Antonius threatens my very existence. If Caesarion ever gains a strong following in Rome, I'm as good as dead."

The old man paused for a moment, choosing his words carefully. "You can stick your sword into Antonius, but the world must believe that the man fell on his own sword out of shame for his failures. His queen can be slaughtered, but the world must believe that she chose to commit suicide instead of suffering capture."

"I see," said Octavian. "There is one version of reality—the private and true version—and there is the other version for all of history."

Claudius nodded. "You must plan your moves carefully. Build the public outrage against Antonius, as you've been doing. Make him extremely unpopular. Then work your way toward a military conflict that you are certain to win. Rome loves a winner, especially if it is one of their own."

Over the next few years, Octavian patiently built outrage and carefully maneuvered Marcus Antonius into a battle he couldn't win.

And the young emperor-to-be followed his advisor's words. He cornered Marcus Antonius, killing him outright, but only amongst his most trusted soldiers.

"Give me his sword," said Octavian. "See?" He took the dead man's sword and shoved it into the same wound that had dispatched him to Elysium. "He committed suicide, falling on his own sword, instead of facing justice. This is how much of a coward was the man who stood against Rome."

All of the officers looking on nodded in agreement. They knew that politics needed to be involved here, every bit as much as warfare.

Later, when Octavian's forces closed in on the Egyptian capital, he pulled his most trusted officers aside and spoke to them in confidence.

"Men, just as Marcus Antonius fell on his sword, his queen must choose the asp for her own death."

"But sire," said one of his generals, "dying by cobra bite takes hours in excruciating pain. She would know that. I doubt—"

"But most people won't know that," replied Octavian. "We need to tell a colorful tale of her ending, otherwise people will suspect the worst of me. That truly would be a tragedy. No, we tell the story that she chose to put her hand in a basket filled with the poisonous vipers. People's thoughts will be so shocked and repulsed, they won't be able to get the picture out of their minds."

"Yes, your eminence," replied the general.

"The age of pharaohs has come to an end," said Octavian. "The age of Roman rule and senatorial wisdom has arrived." He didn't dare speak of himself as emperor. He remembered all too well what had happened to his uncle and adoptive father, Julius Caesar, some fourteen years earlier. He would wait patiently for power to be forced upon him. And he would accept it reluctantly.

Soon, Octavian became known as Augustus Caesar. Though he never proclaimed himself to be emperor, he was that in every way possible throughout the remainder of his life—emperor of Rome and the new ruler of Egypt as a province of that empire.

Conclusion

Modern Egypt looks nothing like its ancient self. It has become a pawn in a far larger game. But if history teaches us anything, we need to remain aware of the patterns of history itself, lest we repeat past mistakes.

By reading this book, you have hopefully gained a fascinating perspective on the gods, monsters, and heroes of Egypt's past. Egypt has had a colorful history. From the deepest reaches of pre-dynastic prehistory through all of antiquity, Egypt has arguably seen more history and culture than any other patch of land on Earth.

If you have enjoyed this book, please be sure to leave a review and a comment! I will take the time to read it. Thank you very much.

Go to

Amazon.com/author/mattclayton

to see more books by Matt Clayton.

Search for "captivating history" in order to find all our history books.

Check out another book by Matt Clayton

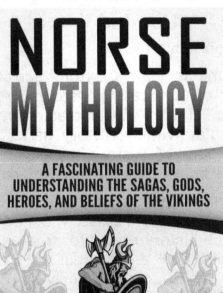

Bonus from Captivating History (limited time)

Hi History Lover!

My name is Matt Clayton, and I'm the creator of Captivating History. First off, I want to THANK YOU for reading my books in the Captivating History series. As an avid reader of History myself, I aim to produce books that will hold you captive.

Now you have a chance to join our exclusive history list so you can get at least one history ebook for free as well as discounts and a potential to get more history books for free! Simply go to

www.captivatinghistory.com/ebook

Also, make sure to follow us on:

Twitter: @Captivhistory

Facebook: Captivating History: @captivatinghistory

If you have any questions; reach out to me by sending an email to **matt@captivatinghistory.com**

CPSIA information can be obtained
at www.ICGtesting.com
Printed in the USA
LVHW080853080821
694774LV00005B/225